KEITH PIRT COLOUR PORTFOLIO

LONDON MIDLAND REGION

Keith R. Pirt

BOOK LAW PUBLICATIONS

Keith Pirt enjoyed putting the rugged scenery of our country as a backdrop to many of his railway slides. Exhaust was also an important element of his subject. Here, both of those things come to the fore as an unidentified Stanier Class 5 has just topped the summit at Ais Gill in July 1966 with an Up freight. Leaving the cutting behind it now begins the descent to Garsdale and at the same time gives some respite to the fireman. BLP - M580.

First published in the United Kingdom by Book Law Publications 2006
382 Carlton Hill, Nottingham, NG4 1JA
Printed and bound by The Amadeus Press, Cleckheaton, West Yorkshire.

INTRODUCTION

This album of Keith Pirt's London Midland Region steam locomotive subjects covers many of the classes still at work during the 1960's. The Settle & Carlisle line provides the location for a number of the views as does the Midland main line through Sheffield, Keith's home town. Suprisingly to some, perhaps, the East Coast Main Line is another venue providing a handful of excellent aspects of LMR locomotives at work. Even the Western Region lines south of Birmingham and along the Welsh border get a look in, albeit with LMS standard classes in the main.

Of course, engine sheds and locomotive works always were good places to photograph engines when they were temporarily static. KRP visited many of those places to give us an insight of the establishments which gave us so much excitement as young trainspotters but which are now seemingly distant memories. Some of the views herein will hopefully bring back some of that nostalgia which we occasionally require as we look back across the gulf of time that seems to widen with each passing decade.

The seasons also played a part in Keith's designs and although winter was one of his favourite, it was usually far from being industrious in producing all the right ingredients at the same moment in time. Nevertheless, we have reproduced some superb pictures here which at the time required hours of lineside patience, in far from comfortable conditions but ideal ones for colour photography.

So, sit back and enjoy another helping of excellent colour photography served up in a variety which will hopefully satisfy the palette but leave the appetite wanting more.

David Allen, Book Law Publications, Nottingham, 2006.

(*opposite*) **Former Whitby based Fairburn Cl.4 No.42083 is captured on film inside the roofless roundhouse at York South engine shed in May 1959. Note that the smokebox door is open and the engine is not in steam, so is perhaps a failure awaiting attention. However, at this time the engine was officially without a home and was more than likely stabled here prior to being reallocated to Sowerby Bridge. This Brighton built 2-6-4T was one of five engines (the others were 42080, 42081, 42082 and 42084) sent new to Stewarts Lane shed during January and February 1951 for working Southern Region local passenger traffic out of Victoria station. It's tenure in London was somewhat short compared with similar engines sent to the SR country sheds, and in March 1952 it transferred to the North Eastern Region where it was to spend the rest of its career until withdrawn. Initially it was allocated to Selby shed but two months later it moved to Scarborough for a short spell on the coast before settling down at Darlington from July 1952 until September 1955. Moving back to the east coast that month, it was indeed a welcome addition to the Whitby allocation until that shed closed in April 1959. When Sowerby Bridge engine shed got it in July 1959, they managed to utilise the engine for two and a half years prior to its last move across Yorkshire to Normanton where for the following five years it worked everything from local passenger services to parcels trains across the Pennines to Manchester. Condemned in April 1967, No.42083 was later sold for scrap. *BLP - M270.***

(*this page*) **With the December chill emphasising the steam, 'Jubilee' No.45566 QUEENSLAND bursts out from under Charlotte Road bridge shortly after departing Sheffield (Midland) with a St Pancras bound express. Based at Leeds Holbeck shed since the early years of WW2, this North British Loco. Co. built 'Jubilee' had started life in August 1934 at Preston motive power depot. In January 1936 it transferred to Patricroft from where, amongst other duties, it was a regular visitor to North Wales. In October 1937 it moved across Manchester to Longsight shed to work the winter season on expresses to Birmingham and London. At the start of the summer timetable in 1938 it went for a couple of weeks to Camden depot before transferring to the Midland Division and a first stint at Holbeck. Shortly after the outbreak of war its was allocated to Derby for three months prior to moving to Normanton of all places. Within days of its arrival at the joint shed, it moved yet again - back to Holbeck from where it worked until withdrawal in October 1962. *BLP - M277.***

Showing off the mixed traffic ability of the class, 'Black 5' No.45063 climbs to Ais Gill summit in apparent ease with a southbound freight in May 1965. The Holbeck based 4-6-0 had spent most of it's British Railways career allocated to sheds in West Yorkshire with Farnley Junction being its favourite depot. It transferred to Holbeck in June 1964 and thereafter worked Midland line traffic such as this both north and south of the city. Withdrawn in October 1966, the engine took one last journey from Leeds in January 1967 - eastwards to Hull and the scrapyard of Albert Draper. Note that the engine still has the lining that had been absent from many engines for a few years prior to this date. *BLP - M241.*

After working in from Buxton with an early morning train, Ivatt Cl.2 No.46480 departs Sheffield (Midland) and starts its return home with a three-coach, all stations, stopper to Buxton in July 1966. The mogul had been allocated to Buxton shed since August 1962 after leaving the North Eastern Region where it had worked since being built at Darlington in October 1951. With nearly ten months of operational life still left before condemnation, No.46480 would continue to serve Buxton shed on duties such as these right up to the end. The cityscape of Sheffield centre makes an interesting background which over the past forty years has changed very little. It is amazing to realise that this scene was captured during the same month that England won the World Cup. *BLP - M252.*

Keith's caption simply states 'Cl.2 46520 in BR green livery, stands under the wires at Crewe, March 1967.' The present writer is not quite sure whereabouts at Crewe this scene was captured nor why the 2-6-0 has white painted buffers and other bits. It has obviously been cleaned, at least above the footplate level. The reporting number board, with what appears to be 1T50 pasted on, has fallen forward. By now based at Northwich shed, No.46520 has just a few more weeks of operational life in front of it before withdrawal, and eventual sale as scrap to J.Cashmore at Great Bridge. One of the former Western Region Ivatt Cl.2s, which in the main were based at Oswestry shed, this engine was put into traffic at Swindon with lined green livery in February 1953. It went to the scrapyard in the same condition. *BLP - M415.*

So, what is the story behind this scene at Rotherham (Masborough) station in July 1956. The Kettering based 8F No.48609 is wearing express headlamp code whilst the carriage stock it is heading is contemporary with express passenger rolling stock. Possibly the answer is that the original train engine was a total failure and had to be taken off the train en route. The only available motive power, suitable or not, was this far-from-home 2-8-0, which was probably at Royston engine shed and from whence it came to the rescue. If any reader knows the full (accurate) story then please drop a line to the publisher. The reader who supplies the most enduring account will receive a book of his/ her choice and that account will be published in a future Pirt colour album as an Addendum. Withdrawn in January 1968 from Patricroft shed, No.48609 had got there in January 1967 via Wellingborough, Leicester Midland and Colwick. *BLP - M419*.

Not quite looking its best but nevertheless holding its own, Hasland based exLMS 2P No.40502 stands in the sun outside Millhouses shed in May 1956 prior to working back to Chesterfield with a stopping passenger train. Even though Hasland shed only had a couple of passenger engines on the books, it was probably not deemed worthwhile for the management to designate labour to clean the engine because the roundhouse there was virtually open to the elements with most of the roof taken down or collapsed because of subsidence caused by local coal mining operations. Formerly a Millhouses engine, No.40502 had moved on to Toton in February 1951 but just over a year later transferred to Hasland. In January 1959 the 4-4-0 was allocated to Nottingham and six months later went further south when Leicester Midland shed beckoned. Within four months it was back at Nottingham where it remained until withdrawn in February 1961. During Midland Railway times this 4-4-0 was designated to work the Royal Train on a number of occasions - how fortunes change. *BLP - M381.*

As late as September 1964 it was still possible to see the surviving members of the 'Royal Scot' class working express passenger trains on the West Coast Main Line. No.46166 LONDON RIFLE BRIGADE, on the eve of its withdrawal, passes Morecambe South Junction with a Down express. Based by now at Kingmoor, this engine, like many others of the class, had certainly been around during its lifetime. When new in October 1930, it went to Longsight for a six year stint. Thereafter it was allocated to Holyhead four times, Longsight for a further three periods, Upperby three times, Camden and Edge Hill each had it twice whilst Holbeck and Kingmoor each had it once. The record goes to Crewe North shed which had it allocated on no less than thirteen separate occasions. When the end came at Kingmoor shed, No.46166 was purchased by West of Scotland Shipbreakers and cut up at their Troon yard. *BLP - M382.*

Newly arrived at Retford in April 1961 after transfer from Boston, Ivatt Cl.4 mogul No.43157 still carries the appendages of its initial operational workings on the Midland & Great Northern Joint. Built at Doncaster and released to traffic in July 1952, No.43157 had its tender fitted with tablet exchanging apparatus for working on the mainly single line M&GN. During the period from 1950 to September 1952, Doncaster turned out about twenty-five of these engines for the M&GN whilst Darlington built another ten. All had tenders fitted with tablet exchange apparatus. Four sheds shared the fleet with Melton Constable having the bulk with Yarmouth South Town, South Lynn and New England having the others between them. When the Midland & Great Northern Joint closed in 1959, the Ivatt Cl.4s dispersed to other areas of the Eastern Region including Stratford, Lincoln, Colwick and Boston. As traffic started to wither and older classes were withdrawn, the Ivatts moved on to pastures a new as in the case of No.43157 to Retford. This engine transferred again in May 1963 to Barrow Hill in Staveley, its last shed before withdrawal in January 1965. It was cut up by T.W.Ward in September 1965 at their Killamarsh yard, which was not too many miles from Doncaster. *BLP - M113.*

Looking very much at home on the East Coast Main Line, 'Duchess' No.46245 CITY OF LONDON climbs Gamston bank with apparent ease whilst hauling a return special from Doncaster to King's Cross in June 1963. Superbly turned out by Camden shed, it's home since it was put into traffic at Crewe in 1943, the Pacific had just a few more month's tenure at the London depot before transferring to nearby Willesden shed. According to the Engine History Card, 46245 resided at 1A until withdrawn in September 1964 but other reliable sources have it down as reallocating to Crewe North shed in July 1964. Whichever history is accurate, the Crimson Lake beauty was relegated to secondary traffic working on its initial move to Willesden and from then on, after a period in serviceable storage during the winter months of 1963, it was downhill all the way to oblivion. *BLP - M109.*

Crewe locomotive works was always a fascinating and exciting place to visit. In March 1959 'Jubilee' No.45659 DRAKE is approaching the conclusion of a General overhaul and has received a new coat of paint that would also be its last. Here, in the company of another 'Jubilee', No.45558 MANITOBA which has yet to visit the paint shop, the engine awaits its tender prior to going back into traffic at Holbeck shed. The Leeds depot was the only home this engine had throughout its life and it was withdrawn from there in July 1963. Only two other 'Jubilees' were ever allocated to one shed throughout their lives: No.45658 KEYES arrived at Holbeck with DRAKE in December 1934, whilst No.45701 CONQUEROR was a lifetime resident of Newton Heath. *BLP - M116.*

Staying at Crewe works, we skip forward in time to May 1964. By now the works were building new diesel electric locomotives of the Brush type 4 variety (Class 47) and many other types were receiving overhauls. Steam locomotive repairs were being slowly wound down but still it was possible to find up to a hundred at the works undergoing various repairs. This view is very representative of that period and reflects the classes of engines being maintained by Crewe: Stanier Cl.5, Stanier Cl.8 and BR 9F. Others getting overhauls included 'Britannia's' and Fairburn tank engines though these latter engines were in the minority. Centre stage here is Nottingham based Cl.5 No.44918 which would finish its days at Trafford Park shed in January 1967. Starred 8F No.48377, of Fleetwood shed, was another 1967 casualty being withdrawn at Heaton Mersey in December of that year. BR Standard 9F No.92122 of Leicester Midland shed ended up, like many of the late surviving 2-10-0s, at Birkenhead and was withdrawn in November 1967. *BLP - M307.*

On the same visit to Crewe in March 1959, Keith Pirt took this shot of one of the works shunting fleet. Ex Lancashire & Yorkshire 'Aspinall' 3F class No.52459 had arrived at Crewe in October 1953 to perform the numerous daily tasks required of the works shunters. Looking fairly clean after a visit to Horwich works for overhaul, the former 'Lanky' 0-6-0 went on working at Crewe until December 1961 when it was condemned. Prior to being allocated to the Crewe fleet, No.52459 had undergone a five-month stay at Rose Grove and before that had been based at Blackpool. Besides this particular 'A' class, the works at Crewe also found employment during the BR period for Nos.52093, 52212, 52218, 52225, 52312, 52345, 52429, 52441, 52464, 52517. For the record, Horwich had employed just two of the class, Nos.52161 and 52275, and then for only a few months each whereas the Crewe contingent worked for many years. *BLP - M125.*

During the BR period the steam locomotives used on the Crewe works shunting job consisted of about ten engines at any one time. However, during the eighteen year period from 1948 to 1966 basically three generations of locomotives were used. Firstly, there was the former LNWR Webb 0-6-0 'Coal Engines' which were replaced in 1953 by the L&YR Aspinall 0-6-0s then, from about 1962, came the LMS 4F 0-6-0. Of course there were a few odds and sods thrown in to the pot such as the pair of Caley saddletanks, the North London 0-6-0T and the LNWR 'Special Tank' No.3323 but these engines were resident at different periods. The last class to make any impact was the 4F 0-6-0 and No.44405 was allocated from February 1963 to withdrawal in June 1966. The allocation history of No.44405 shows a gradual move towards Crewe works which started in February 1952 when it was transferred from Lancaster to Stoke. In July 1958 it went to Alsager then, less than four years later it was into Crewe South shed and within striking distance of the works. Eight months after that it was in and in May 1964, proudly wearing its W12 target board, No.44405 has the weekend off along with the other members of the fleet. It was sold for scrap to Birds Commercial Motors and cut up at Long Marston. *BLP - M328.*

Millhouses 'Jubilee' No.45654 HOOD nears home as it brings a Down express through Dore & Totley triangle having just emerged from Bradway tunnel past the South Junction. After spending most of the BR period of its life allocated to Millhouses shed, it was transferred to Canklow in January 1962 when 41C closed. By March No.45654 left Sheffield for good, or so it was thought, and moved across the Pennines to Agecroft. Finding plenty of employment in the Manchester area at both Newton Heath and Stockport Edgeley engine sheds, the 'Jubilee' carried on working until the summer of 1966. Only eight other 'Jubilees' lasted into 1967. Ironically it did return to Sheffield being cut up at the Beighton scrapyard of T.W.Ward in October 1966 - just thirty years old. *BLP - M425.*

Rose Grove engine shed. The morning sun bathes the fairly clean flanks of resident Stanier 8F No.48441 in March 1967. By now this Lancashire shed was becoming one of the enclaves of working steam on British Railways and would survive long enough to join Carnforth and Lostock Hall as the last working steam motive power depots in the country. The 8F arrived here in February 1966, an orphan from the closed shed at Lower Darwen. It survived until April 1968 when it was condemned. Originally, this engine was one of the wartime Swindon built examples which, when put into traffic in June 1944, went to work on the Great Western at St Philips Marsh shed in Bristol until 'repatriated' to the LMS in 1947. Barrow Hill shed was the recipient but they did not keep it for long and sent it to Goole. In the early 50's it transferred to Northampton and also had a stint at Bletchley. Its first residence in Lancashire was at Dallam shed in Warrington from July 1955. Four years later it went to Birkenhead for a six year period prior to moving to Blackburn. Alongside is one of Birkenhead's grubby 9Fs, No.92123, which was visiting east Lancashire that day and which had played a part in the transfer of 48441 from Merseyside to Lower Darwen as its replacement when the authorities juggled the surviving locomotive types. *BLP - M319.*

19

With the help of the cold, bracing, air to further dramatise its departure, Lostock Hall Cl.5 No.45353 hauls a return excursion away from Blackpool (North) station in spectacular fashion in December 1967. The afternoon sun has caught the event nicely. Arguably, colour photography comes into its own when weather conditions such as this emphasise the working steam locomotive at its grandest. *BLP - M136.*

Besides the little band of narrow gauge locomotives which it employed moving stores around the various shops, Horwich locomotive works had its own dedicated fleet of standard gauge shunting locomotives in the shape of these Aspinall 0-6-0 saddletanks. Crewe works also employed three of the same class, numbered 51412, 51444 and 51446. The Horwich batch comprised five locomotives all of which only ever carried their LMS numbers to withdrawal: 11304, 11305, 11324, 11368 and 11394. In the frame on this day in March 1959 are 11304 and 11394. The latter engine was the first of the bunch to be withdrawn and on condemnation in May 1960 it was, for some reason, towed to Gorton works and cut up there! Notice that both engines have also managed to keep their LMS style smokebox numberplates. Two other BR numbered Aspinall 0-6-0ST worked the Horwich yards in the 1950s, No.51429 which stayed for a number of years and 51496 which lasted on the duty for only a matter of weeks before returning to Newton Heath. *BLP - M200.*

Pictures capturing 'last trains', etc., feature a lot in Keith's work and in this one we see an RCTS special leaving Llandudno Junction for a trip over the Cambrian Lines in July 1962. The 'last' in this picture is the motive power which comprised Stanier Cl.3MT 2-6-2T Nos.40116 and 40078 and were apparently the last of their class to be withdrawn. At the time of this event KRP was not aware of the future but he was canny enough to record this scene and then later on be able to claim 'last'. Both engines were allocated to Bangor shed at the time of the special working and both would be withdrawn during the following November. No.40078 started life at Nottingham shed in March 1935 and over the ensuing years was allocated to sixteen various sheds from Willesden to Macclesfield to Gorton. No.40116 went new to Bournville in July 1935 and it transferred to eleven different sheds over the years ranging from Wellingborough to Bristol to Chester. *BLP - M174.*

With Wild Boar Fell dominating the left skyline, an unidentified and extremely filthy Stanier Class 5 breasts Ais Gill summit with a southbound mixed freight comprising scrap laden wagons and bogie bolsters loaded with steel bars and girders in May 1966. Even though the locomotive is dirty and its number basically illegible, Keith has 'bagged it' because of the nice exhaust and that wisp of steam. The Midland signal box completes the scene. *BLP - M292.*

Another Settle & Carlisle line scene featuring yet another Stanier Class 5 on a northbound freight this time. The engine is No.44912 of Leeds Holbeck, and it is crossing the main road between Sedburgh and Hawes at Garsdale in May 1967. *BLP - M157.*

A recent addition to the Low Moor passenger engine fleet in July 1965 was 'Jubilee' No.45565 VICTORIA which had returned after a four month stint at Wakefield shed. Looking rather clean and particularly smart at the front end, the 4-6-0 is seen in the heart of the Pennines near Luddendenfoot with a return special from Blackpool to Bradford. Amongst the last eight of the active 'Jubilees', VICTORIA was withdrawn in January 1967 and scrapped at Drapers, Hull. *BLP - M214.*

The one hundred and seventy-five LMS 7F 0-8-0 tender engines built at Crewe between 1929 and 1932 were, perhaps, one of the great disappointments of LMS locomotive design. The various reasons behind their failure to perform as designed have been debated time and again. No.49509, seen here languishing at Newton Heath shed in October 1959, was barely thirty years old when condemned in the previous May. It was one of eleven of the class withdrawn that year which left just nine survivors all of which had gone by 1962. The biggest inroad into the class by the breakers' occurred in 1949 when the first withdrawals took place and no less than sixty-one engines were condemned, all of them less than twenty years old. Over the next two years another similar number were condemned and the withdrawals continued every year except 1958 when there was a slight reprieve. No.49509 had been an Agecroft engine when it's withdrawal was announced but it ended up on the 26A scrap line by dint that it was condemned there. The engine started life at Willesden shed in May 1929 along with nine other new 7Fs. In June 1939 it went to Lees shed near Oldham and spent eighteen years there until replaced by a WD 2-8-0. Agecroft shed received it in time for Christmas 1957 but I suppose the staff at 26B did not send a 'thank you' to 26F. Shortly after this picture was taken the 0-8-0 was purchased for scrap by Central Wagon Co. and was cut up at their yard in Ince, Wigan. *BLP - M172.*

Keith Pirt failed to identify the numbers of the locomotives but we are not too bothered because the scene that his camera recorded at Dore & Totley in April 1957 is superb. For the record, the train is the Up THAMES-CLYDE and a Stanier Cl.5 is leading a 'Jubilee'. As can be seen both are making plenty of smoke as they accelerate through the station at about 60 m.p.h. On the Down line another train is 'pegged' for Sheffield or beyond. This classic Midland scene is now a part of history as the station is reduced to a single platform, complete with bus shelter. *BLP - M254.*

Williamthorpe Colliery, Derbyshire, became the last bastion of the LMS 'Jinty' 0-6-0T and in April 1967 No.47289 shunts a rake of NCB wagons toward the washery. No.47289 had been withdrawn from Sutton Oak shed in December 1966 but was reinstated to Westhouses depot the following February so that it could go 'on loan' to the National Coal Board. Another of its ilk, No.47383, withdrawn from Newton Heath shed in December 1966 was also reinstated at the same time to do the same work for the NCB at Williamthorpe. A regular duty for a pair of the small Westhouses 'Jinty' fleet, No.47313 and 47629 were also at work here during 1967. Nos.47289 and 47629 became the last of their class at work prior to withdrawal in October 1967. *BLP - M207.*

Another view of the Williamthorpe Colliery system, this time seen from the opposite side of the line in April 1967 and in the late afternoon. This time 'Jinty' No.47629 has centre stage and is shunting a long rake of empty BR mineral wagons. This is a good vantage point to view the colliery screens in the distance. Unlike No.47289, No.47629 had not been withdrawn and reinstated prior to working the NCB job and, it was no stranger to the area having spent all of it's BR life working around Nottinghamshire and Derbyshire. *BLP - M149.*

The locomotive servicing facility at Williamthorpe Colliery consisted an old Lancashire boiler, visible on the right, converted to serve as a water tank, and the open ground where the ashes were scattered and piled. A timber shed was provided for the enginemen but the locomotives sat outside in all weathers. No.47289 takes a rest whilst No.47313 continues the seemingly endless toil of moving full and empty wagons around this large colliery complex. Williamthorpe merged underground with nearby Grassmoor in the 1950s with the combined production, in excess of 1,000,000 tons most years, coming out via Grassmoor. However, Williamthorpe still had some excellent coal washing and processing facilities hence the amount of coal arriving and departing. Both mines closed in 1970, by which time the 'Jinties' were history. *BLP - M553.*

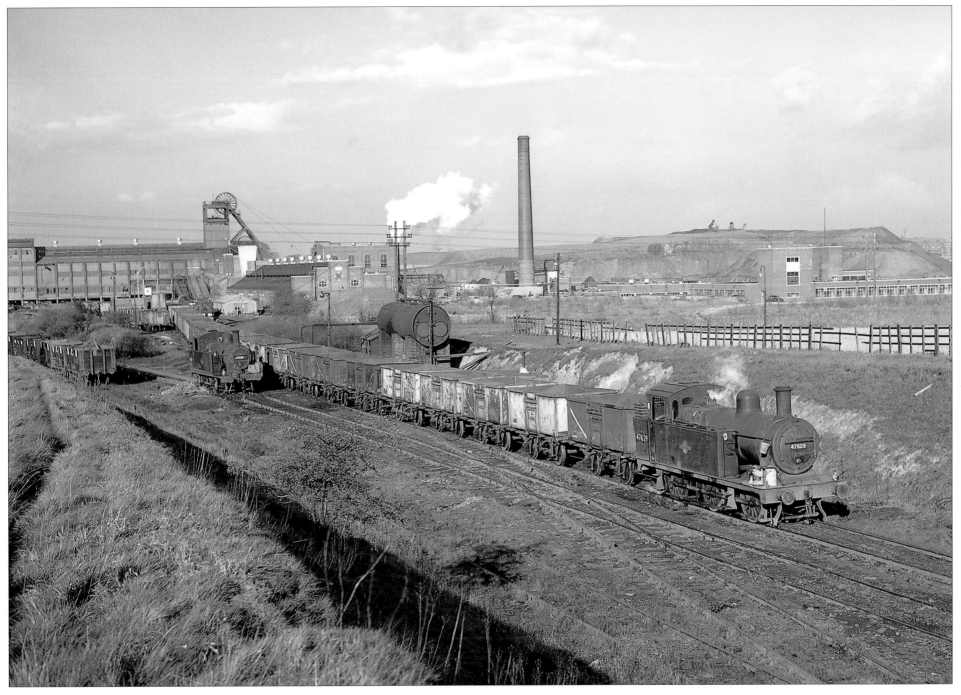

The evening sun in May 1967 lights up the scene at Williamthorpe Colliery as 3F 0-6-0T No.47629 shunts a rake of wagons whilst another 3F stands by. *BLP - M559.*

Putting up a superb exhaust and no doubt annoying some of the residents around Millhouses Park in Sheffield, 'Jubilee' No.45593 KOLHAPUR gets to grips on the climb out of the city with a special for Manchester in April 1967. Another locomotive wearing the yellow stripe on the cabside, this one did not end up in a scrapyard. *BLP - M210.*

This scene could almost be enacted today but it was actually taking place in March 1967. The location is Nappa and the train is a special bound from the Settle & Carlisle for Blackburn. The engines, both Stanier Cl.5s, are 45342 of Carnforth and 45156 AYRSHIRE YEOMANRY of Edge Hill. It is nice to know that they each lasted into August 1968 albeit being condemned on Sunday the 4th. *BLP - M153.*

Taking transparencies inside engine sheds was not always a successful use of film but Blackpool South shed had recently been re-roofed and a vast amount of glass had been incorporated into the structure when Keith captured 'Jubilee' No.45653 BARHAM in April 1959. A long-time resident of Blackpool shed, the 4-6-0 had, since being put into traffic at Camden in January 1935, worked from numerous sheds on the Central, Midland and Western Divisions of the former LMS. It would end its days, as a number of the Blackpool based 'Jubilees' did, at Newton Heath shed. Withdrawn in April 1965, it was purchased for scrap by Drapers of Hull. *BLP - M143.*

No, this scene is not a duplication of M153 on page 33, although the similarities are there. We are still at Nappa but have moved on to August 1968 and this is Cl.5 No.44871 with 44781 (how did that coincidental number combination come about?) working their stint of the last British Railways steam special back from Carlisle. The weather was brilliant but the day was a sombre one in reality, the future uncertain with little prospect of main line steam ever being part of our lives again. How differently things turned out. *BLP - M195.*

Sheffield Grimesthorpe 'Crab' No.42797 has charge of Up special M950 through Millhouses on a lovely sunny morning in August 1957. Where the train was bound for we have little knowledge but it was most probably en route to one of the west coast resorts in Lancashire and would work via the Hope valley line to Manchester thence into L&Y territory. On the shed can be seen an Ivatt Cl.2, a Gresley K3 and a Standard Cl.5. In July 1961 the 2-6-0 moved to Lancaster Green Ayre for a couple of months prior to transferring to Edgeley. Its stay in Stockport was also short because in October it ended up at Birkenhead shed only to be withdrawn during the following March. *BLP - M554.*

The Manchester (Victoria) banking job, or rather more accurately the Miles Platting bank turn, because the banker not only pushed trains from Victoria but also those originating in adjacent Exchange station and, perhaps more importantly, the numerous eastbound freights passing through the station. The banking job used to be the preserve of the Lanky 'A' class 0-6-0s with as many as four engines stabled at busy periods. However, when it actually got busy there would only usually be one stabled whilst the others were pushing a train up the bank or drifting back down after completing another push. By May 1964 the 'A' class was no more so Newton Heath shed supplied anything like this ex Midland 4F or the LMS version for instance. No.43893 was actually based at Skipton, note the tender cab for S&C snow plough duties, so was probably borrowed by 26A (9D by then) for a couple of days. Withdrawn one year after this scene was captured on film, the 4F was sold for scrap to Drapers of Hull. *BLP - M295.*

It was quite rare to see a Stanier Cl.5 on the former Great Northern section of the East Coast Main Line at any time, especially south of Hatfield. However, in August 1961 KRP was there to record No.45116 heading an Up parcels train. Based at Annesley shed during this period, it is unknown why the Vulcan Foundry built Stanier 4-6-0 was utilised for this particular job. For the first twenty-two years of its life, except for the first four months spent at Edge Hill shed, the '5' had worked from Kingmoor shed and had also been on loan to Perth for two months during 1936. In March 1957 it came south to Agecroft and after nearly three years there it transferred to Leicester and worked from the former Great Central shed. Whilst it was on the GC it moved to Annesley in January 1960 for a three-year stint prior to moving on to Kentish Town. The GC beckoned again and Woodford Halse had it 'on the books' for five months. In October 1963 the coast line of North Wales proved to be irresistible and Llandudno Jct. shed became it's home until May 1965 when Mold Jct. shed required it's services. Holyhead called in April 1966 and until Christmas of that year it enjoyed the fresh air of Anglesey. Chester was at the gateway to England from Wales and for the first five months of 1967 No.45116 worked from the former LNWR shed in that city. Finally, Springs Branch in Wigan, not too far from its birthplace, became its last depot and then only for a few weeks as it was condemned in July. This locomotive had certainly been around having worked from depots in England, Scotland and Wales. As if the wanderlust was to stay to the end, the engine was towed to Newport in South Wales and cut up at the scrapyard of J.Cashmore. *BLP - M130.*

The Ivatt LMS Cl.2 mogul first turned out by the LMS in 1946 was a useful and well-liked locomotive particularly at sheds where ancient, open cab, locomotives were the everyday fare of footplatemen. The last examples did not appear until April 1953, a period when the BR Standard classes were being turned out in large numbers. Built initially at Crewe, the class was also built at Darlington and Swindon. The latter 'Western' engines ended up on the former Cambrian lines and many of those, such as No.46512 here, were allocated to Oswestry. This view was taken in the station in August 1963, more than ten years since this engine arrived new from Swindon. A lot of the Western Region based engines were painted in lined green livery and most of those kept that colour to withdrawal. No.46512 left Oswestry in January 1965 for Shrewsbury then, in February, it moved to Willesden. Four months later it was back at Salop but only for a few weeks before it moved on to Stoke. Finally, in June 1966 it transferred to Crewe South shed from where it was withdrawn in November 1966. This locomotive is now preserved. *BLP - M265*.

Looking far from its best 'Duchess' No.46228 DUCHESS OF RUTLAND is seen in July 1964 heading northwards through Farington with a Down parcels train. This was about the lot for the former pride of the LMS locomotive fleet. They had done their work in exemplary fashion but now their time was finished. Their former homes were by now either closed or closing. Nearly half the thirty-eight strong class had already been condemned and scrapped and 1964 was to be the final year when these magnificent machines roamed the WCML. *BLP - M128.*

(*opposite*) 'Jubilee' No.45705 SEAHORSE climbs past Chinley North Junction in June 1965 with a Locomotive Club of Great Britain *THE HIGH PEAK RAIL TOUR* special that is made up mainly of Southern Region stock. At this time the Stanier 6P was allocated to Newton Heath shed for a year having previously resided at Blackpool for the last eight years. Five months after this particular working, the 'Jubilee' was withdrawn, one of thirty-three of the class condemned that year. It was scrapped at Cashmores yard in Great Bridge. *BLP - M140.*

Looking far from resplendent, 'Duchess' No.46246 CITY OF MANCHESTER nears Hartford with a heavy express in June 1959. The last of the class to do so, the maroon Pacific still has the sloping smokebox fitted, giving away the fact that it was once a streamliner. It was soon to enter works for a boiler change and a new smokebox to bring it in line with the other 8Ps. A Crewe North engine at this time, it was reallocated to Camden shed in June 1960 but was one of the early withdrawals, being condemned in January 1963. It was cut up at it's birthplace four months later. *BLP - M215.*

(opposite) **Stanier 8F No.48062** and an unidentified BR Standard Cl.4 climb away from Rose Grove with a heavy ballast train in May 1968. Plenty of slogging here and evidence of re-ballasting is beneath the train. Perhaps these two did not have far to go before the load was lightened. The 8F worked up to the weekend of 4th August when it was condemned along with the other Rose Grove 'survivors'. *BLP - M194.*

What superb nameplates the 'Royal Scots' carried. Not just patriotic, nostalgic and bold, they were big. Big enough for all to see at a station and, as in this case, big enough to see on a locomotive passing the photographer at speed. This is No.46132 THE KING'S REGIMENT (LIVERPOOL) heading a St Pancras bound express from Sheffield past Millhouses engine shed in December 1959. The Kentish Town based 'Scot' had just in fact transferred from Liverpool's Edge Hill shed two months previously after a five-year stay on Merseyside. The Regimental name and badge had been attached to the locomotive in 1936 after it had previously carried the name PHOENIX. This engine was amongst the first of the class to be fitted with 2A tapered boiler and double chimney in 1943. Like most of the 'Scots' it was well travelled and had served twenty various depots over its lifetime. Withdrawn in February 1964 from Carlisle Kingmoor, No.46132 was cut up at the West of Scotland Shipbreakers, Troon in the summer of 1965. *BLP - M178.*

Towards the end of steam working on British Railways, it seemed to be that never a week went by without one service or another being announced as being the last one of its kind to be worked by steam. Local enthusiasts would usually pack the particular train leaving regular passengers and commuters wondering what all the fuss was about? When the last steam hauled Birkenhead to Chester services were run in March 1967 they too were subject to enthusiastic support and Class 4MT No.42587 looks the part as it thrashes through Bromborough with one of the last trains. Birkenhead shed has cleaned up the 2-6-4T to a nice finish but once its passenger work was completed on the Wirral, the Cl.4 went looking for further employment and ended up at Low Moor in April. Alas the work was not there and No.42587 was withdrawn during July. It too ended up as scrap at Drapers. *BLP - M159.*

April 1967, Bingley, West Yorkshire. 'Jubilee' No.45647 STURDEE heads the Down Heysham parcels as one of its last duties, just days before withdrawal. The engine is very clean and we can only surmise that it had been on railtour duty or perhaps the staff at Holbeck shed enjoyed keeping it in this condition. Since being put into traffic in January 1935 at Crewe North, the engine had resided at eight other different sheds over the ensuing thirty-two years. 5A had it on a total of five separate occasions whilst Aston, Bushbury (7 years), Camden, Edge Hill, Farnley Junction, Holbeck, Rugby (12 years), Saltley all had it just once but for some it was longer than most. No matter what the staff at 55A thought about No.45647, six months after condemnation it was cut up in the Great Bridge yard of J.Cashmores. *BLP - M432.*

It is quite amazing how we used to travel, or rather the conditions in which we used to have to travel not too long ago. This picture of Stanier Cl.5 No.45339, of Newton Heath shed, was apparently taken at Easter 1961 alongside the WCML near Euxton Junction, Preston. The train, Central Division excursion C724, is returning from Blackpool to Manchester at a good rate of knots with the engine in fine fettle. However, the carriage stock is made up entirely of non-corridor coaches with neither toilets nor access to them. Now, with no engine failures, engineering or signalling delays or any of the hundreds of other incidents, large or small, which could hold back or delay a train, the journey from Manchester (Victoria) to Blackpool (South, Central or North) took about one hour and twenty minutes - on a good day. Which leads me to the question - how long must a railway journey be, in time, before toilet facilities are provided for passengers. Answers to the publisher please, quoting Midland 439. *BLP - M439*.

Besides being responsible for maintaining all the former Lancashire & Yorkshire locomotives still at work on BR, Horwich works also undertook work on the Ivatt Cl.4 moguls, Stanier 8Fs, the 'Crabs' both Fowler and Stanier types, and some of the LMS designed tank engines. In April 1959 Ivatt Cl.4 No.43112 stands in the yard having just had a 'light' repair and a touch up to its paintwork. The workforce at Horwich would be familiar with this class having built seventy-five of the 2-6-0s in two separate lots from 1947 to 1949 and then 1951-52. No.43112 was amongst the second lot and came into traffic in April 1951 at Skipton shed. At the time of this portrait it was allocated to Lancaster Green Ayre and would remain so until February 1962 when it moved south to Nuneaton. 1962 was an unsettling year for the engine because in June it was transferred to Northampton and then, in October, to Bescot. A year later it went to Stoke and managed a four-year stint there prior to its last move in August 1967 to Crewe South. Shortly after arrival at Crewe it was withdrawn - surplus to requirements - and sold for scrap. *BLP - M422.*

A clean Saltley based Stanier Cl.5. No.45265 heads an Up freight beneath Hatton cutting bridge in March 1962. Evidence of recent remedial abutment work on the east end of the bridge spoils an otherwise classic example of the Great Western Railway multi-arch structures built for this main line so long ago. Ignoring the brickwork, and with a somewhat satisfied comment attached to his notes, KRP simply states - not another cameraman in sight! *BLP - M350.*

Westhouses engine shed in June 1966. The shed was opened by the Midland Railway in 1890 to cater for the growing fleet of 0-6-0 tender engines then required to move coal from the numerous nearby collieries to the expanding Toton yard. The six-road dead-end structure served the steam locomotive until October 1966 when the place was closed to steam but then used as a stabling point for diesel traction. In this view we have a number of the ubiquitous Stanier 8Fs which had gradually taken over from the 3F and 4F 0-6-0s, a solitary BR standard 9F, a 'Jinty' and at least two Type 4 diesel locomotives (Class 47). This busy depot was created to serve the coal industry and as the industry declined dramatically in the mid-1980s, so did the fortunes of this depot. It was closed as surplus to requirements. On view is the elevated coaling stage, a remnant of the 19th Century which was never replaced by a modern coaling plant of any kind. The shed was demolished shortly after BR vacated the site and all trace is virtually gone. *BLP - M538.*

Having already been withdrawn for nearly six months, Fowler 4F No.44278 resides on the 'scrap line' at Westhouses shed in June 1966 waiting for the tow which was soon to transport it to G.Cohen's scrapyard at Kettering. The yellow stripe denotes that it was banned from working south of Crewe on the electrified West Coast Main Line, although having been allocated to Toton shed when it was probably applied makes one wonder as to the necessity of such an adornment. Perhaps the Toton 4F 0-6-0s were back-up motive power for the Westbourne Park power station coal trains that originated from Toton yard (ex Calverton Colliery) and were normally hauled by Stanier 8F and BR Standard 9F locomotives over sections of the WCML south of Northampton. Note that the front numberplate is still in situ although what appears to be a section of the inside motion is resting on the running plate. BLP - M301.

Obviously a regular engine for this turn, 'Jubilee' No.45647 STURDEE again has charge of the Bradford (Forster Square) to Heysham afternoon parcels train in April 1967. This time KRP caught it near Gargrave station in a dramatic setting with a nice exhaust. *BLP - M361.*

Working it's last ever summer, Stanier Class 5 No.45156 AYRSHIRE YEOMANRY, starts away from Morecambe with a return Up special in May 1968. The external condition of the locomotive is immaculate and internally it appears healthy enough. However, the writing was on the wall for this Patricroft based engine and most of the other BR steam locomotives which survived to August 1968. By now the nameplates previously fitted to 45156 had been taken off and superbly painted replicas had taken their place. Subsequent to withdrawal it had one final transfer - which ensured it was there at the end - to Rose Grove shed. *BLP - M555*

Looking somewhat the opposite condition to No.45156 on the previous page, another Class 5, No.44896 of Holbeck shed, works through Bingley with a Down ballast train in June 1967. From new in September 1945, this engine has spent all of its career at Farnley Junction shed until transferring to Holbeck in November 1966. Its demise came in September 1967 at 55A and it was sold for scrap to Cashmores at Great Bridge. *BLP - M556.*

As late as April 1966 it was still possible to find ex Midland built condenser fitted 'Jinties' at work on BR. This is No.47202 on the turntable at Agecroft. Looking rather smart in its clean plain black livery, the 0-6-0T has suffered a mishap to its front bufferbeam which is slightly bent. However, the accident damage did not seem to bother the engine because in August it was transferred to Newton Heath where it worked until the following December. Whether or not the bend was put right I have no idea but I would like to think it was. These MR 3F tanks were, in the main, allocated to former Midland sheds up to the mid-1950s and No.47202 was, for many years during the LMS period shedded at Spital Bridge, Peterborough. Just after nationalisation it returned to Kentish Town then went to Cricklewood from where, in late 1963 it ventured north to Gorton. The following year it spent time at Patricroft and then Horwich works prior to the ten month residence at Agecroft. *BLP - M352.*

We cannot see the banker but the train engines, Stanier Class 5 No.44789 and BR Standard Cl.5 No.73069, appear to be in excellent condition as they head a westbound special over Lydgate viaduct between Todmorden and Copy Pit in May 1968. *BLP - M558*.

The number of exLMS locomotives working over the former Great Western Railway network in the early 1960's was quite astonishing and was something that would have not have been dreamed about ten years previously. In June 1962, Stanier Cl.5 No.44810, another Saltley 4-6-0, heads south with an Up freight over Rowington water troughs in glorious weather. The engine does not appear to be picking up water although by now it could have had a fill and rehoused the scoop. The troughs at Rowington, on the main line between Birmingham and Hatton, were 560 yards long and were commissioned by the Great Western in October 1899. By 1965 with only sporadic use being made of them, it was decided to decommission them and so ended another chapter in the history of GWR steam, although the last locomotive to use the troughs was probably exLMS. *BLP - M231.*

Toton based 8F No.48414 climbs Hatton bank Down loop with a Tyseley bound freight in August 1962. The 2-8-0 was far from its usual stomping ground but this was the period in BR history when locomotives did start to wander far from their normal habitats. However, No.48414 was no stranger to Great Western metals because it started life at Swindon factory in 1943 and was on loan to the GWR from October of that year, when it was allocated to Plymouth Laira shed, until January 1947 when it transferred to the LMS at Royston shed. In July 1947 Cricklewood got it and held on to it for the next twelve years after which Toton claimed it. In April 1965 the 8F was reallocated to Leicester Midland shed but only until the following January when it moved to its last depot - Colwick. In October 1966 it became one of the casualties at the Nottingham shed and was sold for scrap. In effect it had been stationed at sheds formerly owned by three of the Big Four companies - GWR, LMS and LNER. *BLP - M234*.

Permanent Way maintenance and replacement is an ongoing event on the railways as witnessed here outside Manchester (Piccadilly) station in April 1965. The station and its approaches had been got ready for the 25kv electrification and the modernisation that accompanied it a few years prior to this scene being caught on film but the upkeep goes on. Locally based 8F No.48765, from Newton Heath, is doing the honours with the P.W. train which is occupying the lines leading to the former goods station sited alongside the vehicular and pedestrian approach road to the station. Dominating the left background are the former MS&LR and L&NWR grain and goods warehouses which were to disappear in the not too distant future. The catenary on this side of the station supports the 1500 volt d.c. wires of the Manchester - Sheffield via Woodhead route which, in 1965, was still doing good business and extremely busy from both passenger and freight traffic. The 8F was to transfer to Stockport Edgeley shed in November and in September 1967 it moved to another local depot, Heaton Mersey but in May of 1968, on the closure of that depot, it transferred away from the area and joined the other refugees at Lostock Hall. The end for it came on 4th August and it was sold for scrap. *BLP - M354.*

'Royal Scot' No.46115 SCOTS GUARDSMAN in its final British Railways guise, complete with the yellow diagonal stripes on the cabsides. Withdrawn officially on 1st January 1966, the 7P 4-6-0 is seen here at Haworth on the Keighley & Worth Valley Railway in September 1968. The rest, as they say, is history. *BLP - M287.*

During the late 1950s and early 1960s it was not unusual to see lines of derelict steam locomotives either waiting to enter BR works for scrapping or, as was to become a more and more frequent occurrence, waiting to be purchased by one or more of the growing number of private scrap merchants who had begun to take these condemned engines into their yards. This is the 'temporary dump' at Badnall Wharf sidings near Stafford on a late afternoon in March 1959. Prominent amongst the batch of former L&YR and Midland locomotives is 0-6-0ST No.51453, which was withdrawn at Mirfield shed in September 1958. The engine was one of the Barton Wright 0-6-0 tender engines rebuilt at Horwich to tank engine configuration by Aspinall during the last decade of the 19th century. Now, after a very long operational life it has practically come to the end of the road and would soon make a final journey. *BLP - M520.*

Previously in this album page 13 featured saw 'Duchess' No.46245 CITY OF LONDON working Up the ECML back to London with a special in June 1963. However, earlier in the day KRP caught the Pacific on the viaduct crossing the River Idle at Ordsall near Retford, en route to Doncaster. *BLP - M563.*

(*opposite*) Since the days of the London & North Western Railway it had been a regular (daily) occurrence for a Northampton based engine to work to Colwick yard with empty coal wagons. After servicing the engine would haul an ordinary goods train to Doncaster, where the LNWR had their own shed, then work back to Colwick with another goods train prior to working back home with coal. In June 1960, Northampton based Stanier 8F No.48360 was enacting that same sequence and is seen here climbing Gamston bank on the ECML with a Doncaster to Colwick freight on the third and penultimate leg which would take it home. The Horwich built 2-8-0 spent most of its life in the south Midlands being put into traffic at Wellingborough in July 1944. Northampton got it in April 1957 and except for a three month loan to Toton in 1961, kept the engine until June 1962 when it went to Bletchley, its last shed where it was withdrawn in June 1965. *BLP - M221.*

Buxton engine shed on a sunny afternoon in May 1967. This is a view of the yard situated on the eastern side of the depot where half of the resident engines had to brave out the cold winters endured in this area of Derbyshire. By now the allocation of this place was down to just a few classes of steam locomotive with the Stanier 8F being the dominant resident as seen here. The first of the eight-coupled engines is No.48532 which had transferred to Buxton from Newton Heath in October 1965. This engine was to reallocate one more time, to Bolton in early March 1968 when Buxton shed closed on the 4th. However, upon arrival at Bolton it was condemned, probably on account that it was surplus to requirements. The Ivatt 2MT is unidentified but at this time the depot had six of the class in residence (46402, 46480, 46484, 46485, 46492, 46505) and with the exception of No.46480, which was withdrawn in May, all the others were condemned in July 1967. The May 1967 condemnation went to Drapers at Hull to be cut-up whilst the other five were towed down to Newport, Monmouthshire where they were dealt with at the scrapyard of J.Buttigiegs. *BLP - M160.*

(opposite) Just north of Sheffield (Midland) station, in a rock cutting, was Nunnery Main Line Junction, complete with its own signal box. The location was difficult to get to and the day light in this part of Sheffield was not always the brightest. However, once these obstacles were overcome it was a good place to observe trains and photograph them too because the heavy northbound expresses were just setting out after their stop at Midland station so there was usually a fair display of smoke and steam. Bristol Barrow Road 'Jubilee' No.45699 GALATEA has charge of a Bristol to Newcastle express in March 1958 and wears the old green livery. No.45699 transferred to Shrewsbury in September 1961 and was withdrawn from there in November 1964, after which it was purchased for scrap by Woodhams of Barry. Another former Barrow Road 'Jubilee' No.45690 LEANDER was fortunate enough to join GALATEA in Barry and the pair have now been preserved. *BLP - M365.*

Fowler Cl.3 No.40013 stands away on a separate line from its compatriots at Bolton shed in April 1959. Allocated to Newton Heath but stored out of use at Bolton Burnden, this 2-6-2T was still eight months away from being withdrawn but come the New Year of 1960 and it would be condemned along with the others in this scene, No.40065 heads the 'condemned' on the next track. Both of the 3MTs ended up at Doncaster works within weeks of their withdrawal and they were reduced to scrap at 'The Plant'. *BLP - M431.*

'Jubilee' No.45633 ADEN had moved to Preston from Longsight in October 1951 and here at Preston shed, in March 1959, the 6P is looking well looked after. Carnforth acquired the 4-6-0 in September 1961 and then in March 1963 it went to Derby for four months before transferring to its last shed Warrington Dallam in July. Withdrawn in October 1965, No.45633 was sold for scrap to T.W.Ward at Killamarsh. Note the famous landmark behind the coaling plant. *BLP - M171.*

This view of Edge Hill based Stanier Cl.5 No.44906 passing the Dent Down bracket signal in September 1966 with a northbound fitted freight, was captured from the signal box window. The perspective is superb and just goes to show what a fantastic view of the trains the signal 'bobby' actually had. Of course Dent box had some wonderful surrounding views anyway, even before a train came into sight but lets not forget that in winter time, especially during the long hours of darkness, it was a very isolated place and sometimes, in extreme weather conditions, difficult to reach. *BLP - M196.*

In June 1964 the exLMS Pacifics were enjoying their last summer of working and most of the surviving engines had been relegated to the less glamorous and mundane duties such as hauling parcels trains or fitted freights. Needless to say, the majority had a thick coating of grime which a few years previously would have been a rarity. Carlisle Kingmoor shed had acquired 'Duchess' No.46255 CITY OF HEREFORD from nearby Upperby in March 1961 and kept that particular engine fairly clean but for working this Stephenson Locomotive Society special from Carlisle to Leeds, the shed staff put in a bit of extra time and had the engine's green livery looking immaculate which, at this period of BR steam working, was a tribute to their hard work. The Pacific is seen near Bingley with the eleven-coach special after traversing the S&C with ease - a feat which is happily still performed today but certainly undreamt of in 1964. No.46255 was withdrawn on the following 12th September and sold for scrap to Cashmores at Great Bridge. *BLP - M197.*

With the expiry of the 100-year old Agreement between the Midland Railway Co., and the Staveley Iron & Steel Co. looming, 1F 0-6-0T No.41804 still wearing the old BR lion & wheel emblem, shunts pig iron wagons in the Staveley works yard in June 1965. By this time there were five (41708, 41734, 41763, 41804 and 41835) of these 0-6-0Ts engines working the Staveley job, both open and full cab types; all were allocated to Barrow Hill shed for that purpose. In October 1965, when the roundhouse shed at Barrow Hill was closed to steam, they were transferred, on paper, to Langwith Junction engine shed which was geographically nearer to Staveley than the shed where they were actually stored thereafter, Canklow. For more than a year these engines languished at Canklow waiting for the Agreement to expire which at the end of 1966 it duly did. At a stroke all five were condemned in December and four of them immediately sold for scrap. The fifth one, No.41708, was purchased for preservation. *BLP - M286.*

One of the full-cab version 1F 0-6-0Ts employed at the Staveley complex, No.41734, shunts wagons over the weighbridge at the Devonshire Works site in June 1965. Note the lack of a shedplate on the smokebox door. This engine was a relative newcomer to the Staveley Works job and had arrived at Barrow Hill shed in July 1958 from Birkenhead. *BLP - M576.*

Another view of Staveley works with Midland Johnson 1F No.41804 and its load of pig iron trucks, crossing one of the numerous roads criss-crossing the site. *BLP - M545.*

(opposite) **One of the reasons British Railways was losing money at the rate they did is perhaps highlighted here at Ais Gill viaduct in July 1966. Holbeck based Stanier Class 5 No.44854 heads south with the ultimate 'micro' freight.** *BLP - M391.*

How about that for a headboard. With shades of the 1920's and 30's obviously influencing the design of the large circular display, restored former Midland compound No.1000 was also an inspirational choice of motive power for this enthusiast special seen passing Millhouses in September 1961. The writer is not aware of the organisation AMR who had organised the railtour 'Doncaster-York-Darlington' but when those three letter combinations are grouped together there is something of a slight Welsh 'twang' about them. Perhaps the designer remembered the LNER shed codes which had similar abbreviations. *BLP - M222.*

(opposite) One of the last tasks undertaken at Darlington Works prior to closure was the shopping and full overhaul of London Midland Region based exLMS locomotives. On York shed yard in June 1965, Stanier 8F No.48712 of Carnforth depot looks resplendent in what proved to be its last new coat of paint. Note the larger than normal cab side numerals affixed by Darlington. Moving to Rose Grove in May 1967, the 2-8-0 was shortly afterwards withdrawn. *BLP - M285.*

We have all heard of the Skeleton coast, the Gulf coast and the Gold coast but nearer home we have our very own named coastlines such as the Atlantic coast, and the Cambrian coast, etc. This is the Caravan coast or to give it its proper name the North Wales coast. In July 1963 Stanier Class 5 No.45419 heads west along the four-track section of line near Abergele with special 1M34. A recent arrival at Chester LMR depot, the Cl.5 had come from Rugby shed where it had resided since July 1961. *BLP - M550*.

Canklow based Ivatt Cl.4 No.43064 shunts empty carriage stock (note the new Mk.1 coaches) on the Up main at Heeley carriage sidings, Sheffield in June 1965. This view shows the 2-6-0 during its last few days of work because by the end of the month it was withdrawn after a transfer to Langwith Junction depot. This was one of the initial batch of twelve that went new to New England shed for work on the M&GN line and other parts of the Eastern Region. Doncaster built, it came into traffic in November 1950. Transferring to Boston in December 1957, after a stint at Spital Bridge and later New England again, it enjoyed five years in Lincolnshire prior to moving to Colwick in January 1963. In October 1964, in a bid to chase what little work was available for such a useful engine, No.43064 basically ended its days at Canklow on duties such as this. *BLP - M169.*

Farnley Junction based 'Jubilee' No.45581 BIHAR AND ORISSA appears to be in reasonably clean condition on York shed yard in April 1965 after working in from Leeds. This 6P still had another eighteen months of work in front of it during which time it became a regular on excursions to the holiday resorts on the west coast and for hauling enthusiast specials. *BLP - M213.*

Wellingborough shed was not renowned for its Stanier Cl.5 allocation and the only time the depot ever had any 'on the books' was in December 1944 when 4823 and 4824 went new from Derby works, whilst 4856 and 4857 arrived new from Crewe. All four engines left 15A during August 1945 and no other Cl.5 was ever shedded there again. So, No.45221 must have been a visitor on shed for servicing in September 1957 and indeed it was because it had been a Bedford based engine since the previous January. During its thirty-two year life, No.45221 moved no less than twenty-two different times and ended up at Edgeley shed where it was withdrawn in December 1967. *BLP - M219.*

Euxton Junction, March 1961, with Stanier Cl.5 No.45318 heading south with an express. We have no idea of this particular working but the Blackpool based 4-6-0 has a long and interesting set of rolling stock in tow. It is fairly late in the afternoon so it is not one of the Blackpool-Manchester 'Club' trains which left the seaside in the morning with the return in the early evening. The engine itself, one of the 300-odd produced by Armstrong Whitworth, had a somewhat interesting career since being put into traffic at Bangor shed in February 1937. In January 1940 it moved to Llandudno Junction shed but only for three months before it was called to Crewe North where it spent the rest of the wartime years. In May 1945 it transferred to Shrewsbury for a six year stay. In August 1951, just to prove it was a truly cosmopolitan locomotive, it was allocated to St Margarets shed in Edinburgh. After two years north of the Border it returned to England and Blackpool Central shed became it's home for the next eleven years. Just prior to that establishment closing in November 1964, No.45318 transferred away to Bury in September and spent the winter there. Bolton was its next depot and from April 1965 to July 1968 it earned a living which kept it going to the end. The end came at Lostock Hall depot on 4th August 1968 and to complete the cycle it was towed away to Hull where scrap metal dealer Albert Draper reduced it to small pieces of metal ready for the furnaces. *BLP - M227.*